info@kinfolkmag.com
www.kinfolkmag.com

Printed in the United States of America

Publication Design by Amanda Jane Jones
Cover photograph by Tec Petaja
Cover Stylist Chelsea Petaja

weldon**owen**

415 Jackson Street, Suite 200,
San Francisco, CA 94111
Telephone: 415 291 0100
Fax: 415 291 8841
www.wopublishing.com

Weldon Owen is a division of

BONNIER

KINFOLK

SUBSCRIBE

VISIT SHOP.KINFOLKMAG.COM

FOUR VOLUMES EACH YEAR

CONTACT US

If you have any questions or comments,
email us at *info@kinfolkmag.com*

SUBSCRIPTIONS

For questions regarding your subscription,
email us at *subscribe@kinfolkmag.com*

STOCKISTS

If you would like to carry *Kinfolk*,
email us at *distribution@kinfolkmag.com*

SUBMISSIONS

Send all submissions to
submissions@kinfolkmag.com

WWW.KINFOLKMAG.COM

WELCOME

Taste, sight, sound, touch, and smell. We experience everything around us through our senses, and while this fall volume continues to share stories of entertaining, community, and shared tables, it also explores ways to refine those senses, as a way to enrich the experiences we have with each other. Kathrin Koschitzki's photo essay, "Leaving," documents her personal challenge to see the leaves in her neighborhood with a new perspective. Andrea Gentl and Martin Hyers focus on the overlooked messes that linger after cooking in our kitchens with "Apron Recipes," and Amy Merrick converts a dusty garage into a refreshing space for drying fragrant herbs. Nico Alary and Sarah Lang both write of coffee brewing methods that slow and enrich the experience, while Kirstin Jackson shares a homage to cheese, praising not only the taste but the role of cheese in our lives.

You'll notice that we have also decided to weave recipes throughout this and later volumes. While there are, of course, great resources for recipes elsewhere, we'd like to share a few of our favorites along with the images and stories we love.

Leonardo da Vinci, the Renaissance man of unquenchable curiosity, reflected that the average person "looks without seeing, listens without hearing, touches without feeling, eats without tasting, moves without physical awareness, inhales without awareness of odor or fragrance, and talks without thinking."[1] We hope to share more meals together this autumn, and plan to heighten our sensory awareness of at least a few more details—the wonder contained at the table, in the outdoors, in the people around us—to challenge Leo's glum assessment and, well, enjoy ourselves a bit more while we're at it.

NATHAN WILLIAMS, EDITOR OF KINFOLK MAGAZINE

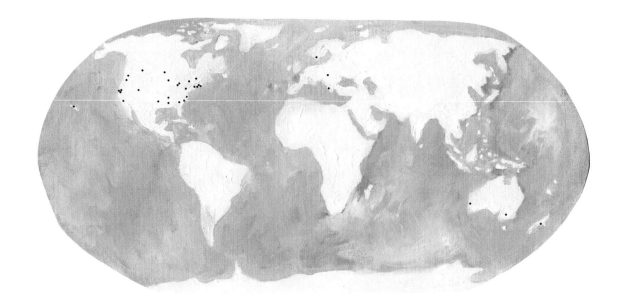

NATHAN WILLIAMS
Editor
Portland, Oregon

AMANDA JANE JONES
Designer
Ann Arbor, Michigan

DOUG BISCHOFF
Sales & Distribution
Portland, Oregon

JULIE POINTER
Features Editor & Gatherings
Portland, Oregon

KATIE SEARLE-WILLIAMS
Features Editor
Portland, Oregon

NATASHA MEAD
Design Assistant
New Zealand

ERICA MIDKIFF
Copy Editor
Birmingham, Alabama

PAIGE BISCHOFF
Accountant
Portland, Oregon

CARISSA GALLO
Photographer
Portland, Oregon

KATIE STRATTON
Painter
Dayton, Ohio

ANDREW GALLO
Film Maker
Portland, Oregon

AMY MERRICK
Florist & Writer
Brooklyn, New York

PARKER FITZGERALD
Photographer
Portland, Oregon

NIKAELA MARIE PETERS
Writer
Winnipeg, Canada

JESSICA COMINGORE
Online Editor
Los Angeles, California

KATHRIN KOSCHITZKI
Photographer
Munich, Germany

CAROLINE EGAN
Writer
San Francisco, California

SARAH LANG
Writer
Madison, Wisconsin

GENTL & HYERS
Photographers
New York, New York

AUSTIN SAILSBURY
Writer
Copenhagen, Denmark

CHANTELLE GRADY
Photographer
Montreal, Canada

JASON HUDSON
Writer
Toronto, Canada

NICHOLAS J KOCH
Writer
San Francisco, California

JENICE LEE
Stylist
Seattle, Washington

HEIDI SWANSON
Writer
San Francisco, California

CHRISTINE WOLHEIM
Stylist
San Francisco, California

JOEL CLARE
Film Maker
Seattle, Washington

NICO ALARY
Photographer & Writer
Victoria, Australia

KRISTINA GILL
Photographer & Writer
Rome, Italy

JULIE WALKER
Film Maker
Salt Lake City, Utah

WON MCINTOSH
Writer
Jackson Heights, New York

WE ARE THE RHOADS
Photographers
Seattle, Washington

MATT WALKER
Film Maker
Salt Lake City, Utah

ALEXIS SIEMONS
Writer
Philadelphia, Pennsylvania

KRISTOPHER ORR
Photographer
Alberta, Canada

BETH MURPHY
Writer
San Diego, California

ALICE GAO
Photographer
Brooklyn, New York

LAURA DART
Photographer
Portland, Oregon

LARISSA MURPHY
Writer
Indiana, Pennsylvania

AGATHA KHISHCHENKO
Writer
Brooklyn, New York

ERIN SCOTT
Photographer & Writer
Berkeley, California

KIRSTIN JACKSON
Writer
Oakland, California

TIM ROBISON
Photographer
Asheville, North Carolina

MICHAEL GRAYDON
Photographer
Toronto, Canada

KRISTINA TOSI
Recipe Writer
San Francisco, California

ANGHARAD BAILEY
Stylist
Brooklyn, New York

NIKOLE HERRIOTT
Photographer
Toronto, Canada

DANICA VAN DE VELDE
Writer
Perth, Australia

ALEX FARNUM
Photographer
San Francisco, California

TEC PETAJA
Photographer
Nashville, Tennessee

MICHAEL MULLER
Photographer
Austin, Texas

LISA MOIR
Stylist
San Francisco, California

CHELSEA PETAJA
Stylist
Nashville, Tennessee

ALPHA SMOOT
Photographer
New York City, New York

FEW

ONE

ENTERTAINING FOR ONE

○

IN SEARCH OF HOME

A move to a different continent brings new perspectives on home—
past, present, and future.

WORDS BY AUSTIN SALISBURY & PHOTOGRAPHS BY MICHAEL GRAYDON
STYLING BY NIKOLE HERRIOTT

Somehow "home" is broad enough to be a city and narrow
enough to be two bedrooms and a bath.

As I write this we are, for the moment, homeless. It is probably more accurate to say that we are "houseless" or "between homes." In a few weeks we are moving from the US to Denmark, but for now we are in transition: travelers on the open road. We have already shipped away the contents of our first house, and we know we have closed a chapter that can never be reopened. You only get one first house as husband and wife; ours was old and painted green and full of beginnings. But now we are forging ahead, together, into an entirely new chapter.

Before we make the big move across the Atlantic, we are visiting some of the towns where we used to live—a farewell tour of sorts. We are spending time with family and friends, seeing the houses we remember, and visiting favorite haunts from our past. We are time travelers, stopping momentarily into each other's childhoods, alight with fond memories and old stories. *This is the house where we lived…Katie was so tiny back then…I learned to swim in that river, but it was bigger then, I think.* On the miles of open road between our destinations we are finding ourselves revisiting a million memories of the past and present, and talking about the future of what it means to be home.

Home. It's a loaded word with a menagerie of meanings—commercialized, politicized, and romanticized. Few other ideas inspire such diverse emotions, such varied understandings, or such personal interpretations as the word "home." Perhaps only the words "love" and "God" come close in their complexity, and for the same reason: they represent ideas that are too big for words. Somehow "home" is broad enough to be a city and narrow enough to be two bedrooms and a bath. For some, home represents the utopia of a happy childhood, a time and place of safety and nostalgia, a place they might return to if they could. For others, home is the reality of a dark past, an inverted nightmare, something to continue running from. But for all of us, home is multi-dimensional—it is many things.

We all have, of course, the place we now dwell and work and commune—our own friends and geography. This is often different from the place that we came from: our parents and their houses, the high schools we spilled out of, and the towns that helped raise us. For those of us who now live away from our hometowns, or the places our parents or families live, we exist in a kind of perpetual duality, building new lives in new places but also tethered to something old and familiar and rich with history. This duality, complicated by distance, can create a tangible tension between the love of two homes—the one from which we came and the one we are trying to make. This tension is a cocktail of love, reminiscence, regrets, affection, aspiration, fear, and pride. We have always longed for our liberty, and because of that, we often undervalue

We have always longed for our liberty, and because of that, we often undervalue where we come from. But this is "growing up" or "making our way in the world," this weaving together of old and new, this keeping the best of what made us who we are and, yet, making something of our own.

where we come from. But this is "growing up" or "making our way in the world," this weaving together of old and new, this keeping the best of what made us who we are and, yet, making something of our own.

As we've trekked through the cities and states of our farewell tour, I am continually reminded that home is the result of intersecting lives. It is the secondary color created by individuals in relationships. When we speak of our hometowns, what we really mean is, "The place where my sisters and I grew up," or "The place I met my first best friend," or "The place where my kids were born." Yes, home is the landscape of people, places, and things upon which we live out life—but it is mostly about the people. That is why home can be a suburban neighborhood, or a struggling farm, or a ship at sea, or a war-torn nation. After all, home is where hearts are.

Earlier this month, when we packed up all our things, the whole of our combined worldly possessions could be measured in thirteen curated boxes of life: boxes of the things we've

bought or found or made together over the past few years. By themselves, they are not a home, but these few things are a part of us, so they get to tag along. And we, like our boxes, are time capsules being reassigned to life on a new continent, in a new city, in a new neighborhood, and eventually in a new house. There, across an ocean, within the walls and under the roof of some yet-to-be discovered abode, we will reside; we will gather with friends as well as retreat from the noise of the world. Over time we will laugh and share and struggle and whisper that future house into something that breathes—something alive.

We are sure that we appreciate the art of "making home" only because our individual families before us did it so well—though incredibly differently—and because they gave us the raw material for the home we are making together. From those people, places, and things that raised us we learned to keep the best of what we were given and craft it into something brand new. And so, for the next while, our home goes to Scandinavia: man, wife, belongings, and the belief that home exists wherever it is that we are together. ○

THE PERFECT CUP: MATT PERGER

A barista from one of Melbourne's busiest cafés sits down to discuss cupping as a coffee brewing method at home.

A BREWING SERIES BY NICO ALARY

As we wait for it to decant and cool, he explains that he loves coffee because he will never fully understand it, never master it, no matter how hard he tries.

I've been trying to live in many different cities over the last eight years, looking for somewhere I would be comfortable calling home. I have lived here and there for a few months, sometimes years, and my favorite part of the search has been meeting people. I think you can value the quality of a city by the people who populate it.

I now live in Melbourne, and was happy to meet Matt Perger, who oversees many aspects of ST. ALi, one of the busiest cafés in the city. When I ask if he's interested in contributing to this brewing series, he suggests we discuss cupping as a home brewing method. I immediately agree.

It's a Wednesday and I can hear the familiar clicking of my front gate. I walk down the long corridor, typical of Melbourne's terrace houses, and invite Matt in. He has brought a fresh bag of Colombian coffee that he roasted just the day before. As I start taking photos, Matt methodically weighs and grinds the beans, medium-fine. When the kettle is ready, he transfers the grounds to a ceramic bowl and pours the hot water in, creating a circular swirl.

A beautiful crust forms on top of the bowl and the comforting scent of freshly brewed coffee fills the kitchen, mixing with the smell of buttery *croissants* I'm slowly warming in the oven. After four minutes, Matt breaks the crust and removes the top layer of coffee grounds to prevent further extraction. As we wait for it to decant and cool, he explains that he loves coffee because he will never fully understand it, never master it, no matter how hard he tries.

We start ripping generous chunks off the buttery *croissants*, talking about how coffee is a fruit—the seed of the coffee cherry—and, like many fruits, is the most delicious when fresh. I take my first sip of the silky black cup; it is amazingly sweet and clean and tastes like caramelized plum. Matt smiles; he loves to make coffee for others, to show people how good it can be. As we finish the *croissants* and drink the last of our coffee, I am thankful for the great people I've met throughout my travels, and realize that I might have finally found home. ○

CUPPING METHOD

INGREDIENTS

3 ½ ounces boiling water

1 tablespoon coffee,
ground medium to coarse

METHOD

This makes coffee for one.

Any size of bowl or mug works well for brewing. Just use a half of a tablespoon of coffee for every 3 ½ ounces of water.

Measure 1 tablespoon of coffee that has been ground medium to coarse, and tip grounds into a ceramic cup. Pour 7 ounces boiling water over the grounds, ensuring they all get wet.

Wait 4 minutes.

Gently break the crust with a spoon, getting close to enjoy the smell. Remove the foam and decant into a mug, leaving the coffee grounds behind.

Enjoy.

AUTUMN TRADITIONS

WORDS BY DANICA VAN DE VELDE

In "Day and Night Songs," Irish poet William Allingham beautifully describes autumn as "the mellow time."[2] Indeed the shift into autumn's tastes, textures, and colors is mellow. The palette becomes one of deep mauves, yellows, and oranges; the food becomes warmer and more comforting; there is a feeling of settling down slowly. Autumn, a season of warmth and contentment, is inspiration for many traditions in my home.

AUTUMN CLEANING Spring cleaning is a well-established custom for many, but I find the prospect of autumn cleaning far more enticing. Replacing the cotton shorts and t-shirts of summer with woollen scarves, mittens, and beanies is a tangible representation of the shift into my favorite season. Just as the landscape is touched with the earthy reds, yellows, and oranges of autumn foliage, I place snuggly throws on sofas and wrap scarves around my neck.

AFTERNOON WALKS As a young girl I participated in a number of scavenger hunts, collecting as many types of flora as possible. Although my childhood scavenging days are well in the past, I still cannot resist an imperfectly formed pinecone or the delicate texture of a fallen leaf. For me, that point in the afternoon when dusk begins to settle and the crisp air tinges your cheeks a rosy shade of pink is the best time to experience the natural magic of the season.

HOT FROM THE OVEN I bake year-round; even through the sweltering heat of summer, I will endure the almost intolerable sultriness of my kitchen for a home-cooked meal or treat. With the cool change of autumn, however, the warmth of baking brings its own pleasure. Whether I'm making my favorite peanut-butter-and-chocolate-chip cookies or Finnish rye bread, the delicious scent of baking that fills the house—combined with the cozy heat from the oven—is one of the unassuming treasures of the transition into chilly weather.

CULTIVATING THE WINTER HERB GARDEN While gardening is commonly associated with the spring, when the earth is regenerating, I always plant new herbs in my garden for the onset of autumn. As summer herbs such as basil, coriander, and parsley wilt and fade away in the cooler months, I replace them with hardy herbs that can withstand the harsh changes to the climate. Harvesting rosemary, sage, and thyme for roasting meat and flavoring root vegetables is a quintessential autumn activity in my house.

THE INDOOR PICNIC Although picnics are usually linked with the more temperate seasons, there is something to be said for subverting the *al fresco* nature of picnicking when it is either too cold or too wet to be outside. Setting up an informal picnic blanket and cushions on the floor of the living room is one of my favorite ways of gathering with friends. A simple *mezze* (selection of Greek appetizers), a homemade music compilation inspired by the changing season, and good company are all that is required.

THE CAFÉ STROLL Balzac once claimed that the act of strolling is "*la gastronomie de l'œil*" or "the eye's gastronomy,"[3] shedding light on how the sights of the urban and rural environment can provide nourishment. Taking this idea a step further, a few of my close friends and I regularly indulge in what could be termed a café stroll. We spend the day wandering through inner-city neighborhoods in search of hidden nooks, and we pause to warm our toes and sate our appetites with milky lattes and rich hot chocolates.

SOMETHING NEW As much as the familiarity of time-honored rituals brings a sense of reassurance and comfort, there is undoubtedly something special about adopting new traditions. I recently had my first taste of mulled wine, fragrant with star anise, cinnamon, nutmeg, cloves, and citrus, and I was instantly won over. The feeling of a slower pace in autumn provides time to cultivate different approaches to the everyday and to make small changes to our seasonal repertoire. I may try making *gnocchi* for the first time or learn how to knit, but I will definitely be spending my evenings stirring spices into a saucepan of gently simmering red wine.

MAKING SOUP During the '80s and '90s, handwritten recipes regularly circulated in my mother's office. As I became increasingly interested in food, I often found myself leafing through the folder that contained those beautifully scrawled memories of shared meals. The one recipe to which I still turn is cream of pumpkin soup. Originally made by my mother's best friend, Moira, the golden hue of the soup with its swirled flourish of cream and sprinkling of parsley—a food signature of many '80s dishes—is not only immediately evocative of the season, but also gestures toward the subtle inheritance of food traditions. ○

HERB DRYING

Cut, hang, dry—it's a straightforward thing to collect herbs for cooking.
In a fall ritual for gardeners and cooks alike, plants are ferociously clipped at their peak to
save for future cooking. We turned a friend's dusty garage into an herb-drying shed as
a way to celebrate the end of the growing season.

WORDS AND STYLING BY AMY MERRICK & PHOTOGRAPHS BY PARKER FITZGERALD

Cold-weather food demands herbs. Savory tarts, stews, and roasts all beg for them in the same way a chilly night begs for an extra pair of socks. In early fall, herbs are rioting with growth and the kitchen's demand for them also increases. The thought of winter's first frost is all it takes for us to descend, clippers in hand, to save some of the bounty for the months to come. Home-dried herbs are fresher and more satisfying to cook with, and the process is nice way to welcome fall.

Herbs can be gathered from a kitchen garden, a windowsill, a fire escape, or a big container on the front stoop. Otherwise, they can be foraged, begged or bartered for, or simply bought. We did a little bit of each when we turned the unused garage into an herb-drying shed during a rainy Portland weekend. Our lavender came from a massive, unruly planting in an abandoned parking lot, and bits of the rosemary were from someone's street-side bush that had overtaken the sidewalk. Handfuls of mint came from the backyard, and a friend who helped with the hanging brought bunches of sage from her garden. The oregano and thyme and more rosemary were bought the old-fashioned way, cash in hand, from a grower.

It took two days to clean the garage; piles of plywood were removed, paint was scraped, and boards were bleached. Windows were washed and spider webs swept. We made short work of it and strung up several rows of twine, nearly at the ceiling, pulled taut—the weight of fresh herbs will cause the twine to sag, so the higher the better. Bunches were rinsed and dried, with a few inches stripped from the bottom of each stem, and then bundled and strung along the rows.

The best part of the project, more than the herbs we dried or the photos we took, was seeing the potential in an unassuming space and creating something unexpectedly beautiful there with a friend. With our bunches piled high, the smell of rosemary and sage were strong to the point of distraction and we couldn't help feeling like we'd been transported to a cottage in the English countryside. I'd catch him face-deep in a bunch of lavender and I couldn't stop

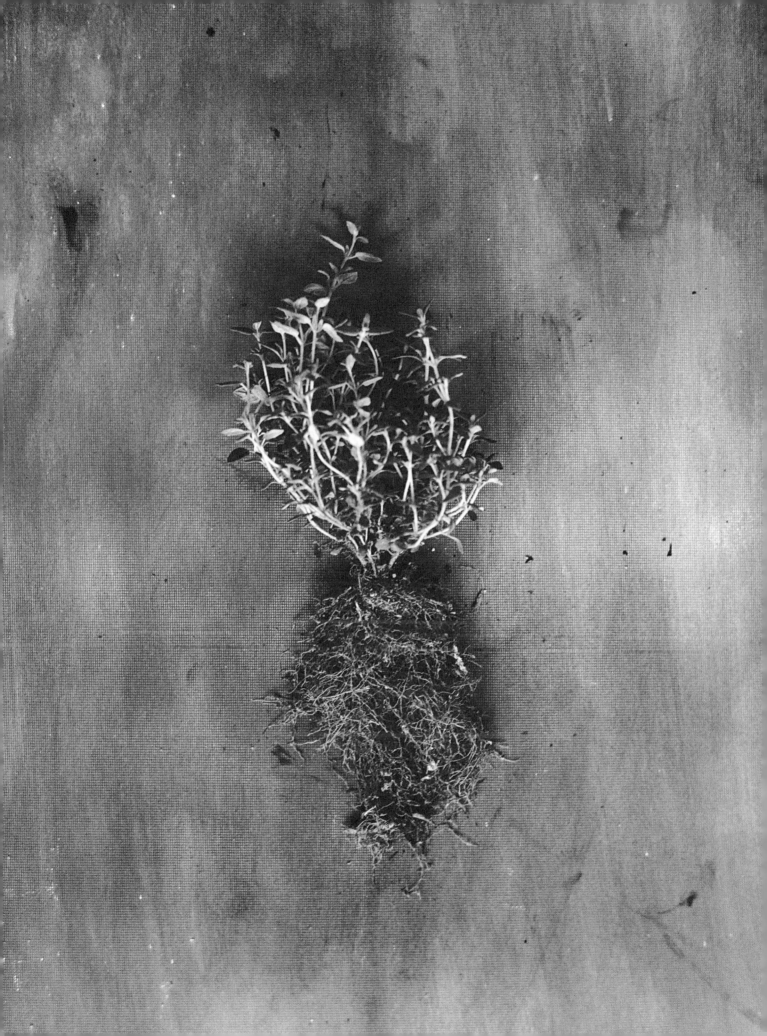

We didn't have to fill the garage with dozens of beautiful bunches;
we could have tied a small row of herbs across the kitchen window or dangled
a single strand over the sink.

rubbing sage between my fingers. That weekend, every shirt pocket held a stray piece of rosemary and every canvas tote collected lavender buds. Even his truck's rearview mirror got its own tiny bunch of thyme, and I couldn't stop myself from crushing bits to smell every time we ran an errand. Meanwhile, Burnside Avenue still rushed past the front door, and we were surprised to find ourselves on a busy street in Portland when we stepped outside.

When the herbs dry (it takes just a week or two), they can be bottled up or left hanging, with pinches broken off as needed. Doing a bit of both is a good compromise; the bottles keep the herbs fresh and the hanging bunches keep a house cozy. Uses are as varied as the herbs that can be dried: teas can be brewed, treats baked,

meats rubbed, and vegetables seasoned. The usual suspects of rosemary, sage, thyme, and oregano are all indispensible, but marjoram, dill, bay, chamomile, lavender, and summer savory add variety to a kitchen throughout the colder months.

We didn't have to fill the garage with dozens of beautiful bunches; we could have tied a small row of herbs across the kitchen window or dangled a single strand over the sink. We could have used the dregs from a grocery store bundle, after the bunch had been unceremoniously stuffed in a glass to keep from wilting. The act of gathering and saving, and the foresight it takes, is more important than scale or provenance. It's a simple process: cut, hang, dry. And when you're ready get to the heart of the matter, cook. ○

LEMON SPICED PEAR

FORAGED HERBAL TEA RECIPE BY ALEXIS SIEMONS

As we settle into fall winds and winter chills, we often seek comfort in steamy sips. Reach for the summer harvest of dried herbs and flowers tucked away within the cabinet for an herbal infusion. Be sure to bring cold water (preferably filtered) to a full boil before steeping to help extract the oils lingering within the dried petals and leaves. If you don't have a small teapot and infuser in your kitchen collection, simply use a large, unbleached paper filter bag (Finum brand recommended) in a pot on the stove. From spiced lemon flavors to the delicate depth of floral notes, these recipes are sure to soothe your mind, body, and soul from the cold and awaken summer garden memories. *Serves 2.*

2 ½ cups cold water, preferably filtered
1 teaspoon dried lemon thyme
1 teaspoon dried lemon verbena
1 teaspoon dried lemon balm

1 tablespoon fresh ginger, thinly sliced
4 tablespoons fresh pear, finely chopped
1 teaspoon wildflower honey

METHOD Heat the cold water to a full boil. Place the lemon thyme, lemon verbena, and lemon balm into the infuser of a small teapot. Pour the boiling water over the herbs and let steep for 5 minutes while covered. Remove the infuser; reserve herbs and flowers for a second steep.* Add herb-infused liquid to a pot on the stove over medium heat and bring to a boil. Add ginger and pear and reduce heat to low. Simmer for 15 minutes. Remove ginger and pear, and stir in honey. Serve in two cups while still steaming.

* Increase second steep time to 6 minutes.

CARDAMOM BLOSSOMS

FORAGED HERBAL TEA RECIPE BY ALEXIS SIEMONS

The delicate, smooth, floral flavors of chamomile and lavender flowers perfectly pair with aromatic orange blossom water, and are brightened by the sweetness of mint and the earthy, citrus notes of cardamom. *Serves 2.*

---

2 cups cold water, preferably filtered
1 teaspoon dried mint
1 teaspoon dried lavender flowers
1 teaspoon dried chamomile flowers

1 teaspoon green cardamom pods, crushed
(steep both seeds and pods)
½ teaspoon orange blossom water

METHOD Heat the cold water to a full boil. Place the mint, lavender flowers, chamomile flowers, and crushed green cardamom pods and seeds into the infuser of a small teapot. Pour the boiling water over the herbs and flowers and let steep for 7 minutes while covered. Remove the infuser; reserve herbs and flowers for a second steep.** Add a splash of the orange blossom water and stir. Serve in two cups while still steaming.

** Increase second steep time to 8 minutes.

A SLOWER CUP

A couple reflects on the slow and methodical brewing technique that allows them to spend time together and offers a relaxed start to their day.

A beverage as alluring, delicious, and influential as coffee should be savored. If prepared correctly, it adds so much to the morning meal, the time of day that offers us a brief but important chance to prepare our bodies and minds for what's to come. My husband and I savor the sun poking its rays through our windows, the robins and finches celebrating the new day, the last sips of coffee before heading out into the world.

Many people only have time for coffee as they rush out the door. It's not thoughtfully enjoyed, but merely consumed. For them, it is a necessary evil, an abused drug, and its job is only to awaken, to dilate, to encourage us out of our slumber so we can face the feverish pace of the workplace. Their ritual consists only of pressing a button.

My husband and I prepare our coffee in a siphon coffee maker. The method was devised in the late 1800s, and was a popular brewing method until the mid-twentieth century. The siphon is immersive and intentional. It's controlled chaos. The teakettle whistles away, informing us that the water is ready. We hand grind the beans, a sound that is harsh but enticing. A small burner's flames lick the base of the siphon's flask, forcing hot water into the top flute. We add the grounds and stir, watching them swirl around inside the chamber. After just over a minute we snuff out the flame. As the flask cools, its vacuum forces the coffee from the top flute back down into the base. We are forced to slow down, to wait, to enjoy the gift of morning.

For my husband and me, it's not the coffee that unfurls our minds and spirits, but the meaningful conversation that accompanies it. It's not the coffee that lifts our eyes and awakens our bodies, but the time we take to make it. And it's not the coffee that prepares us for the day, but the encouraging words from those we love.

Siphon coffee is a beautiful sensory experience, but more importantly it's a part of our routine, one that calls us together to sit and stay a while. And for those times when we drink it alone, it offers an opportunity for quiet reflection, a moment of clarity before we start our daily journey.

WORDS BY SARAH LANG & PHOTOGRAPHS BY CHANTELLE GRADY

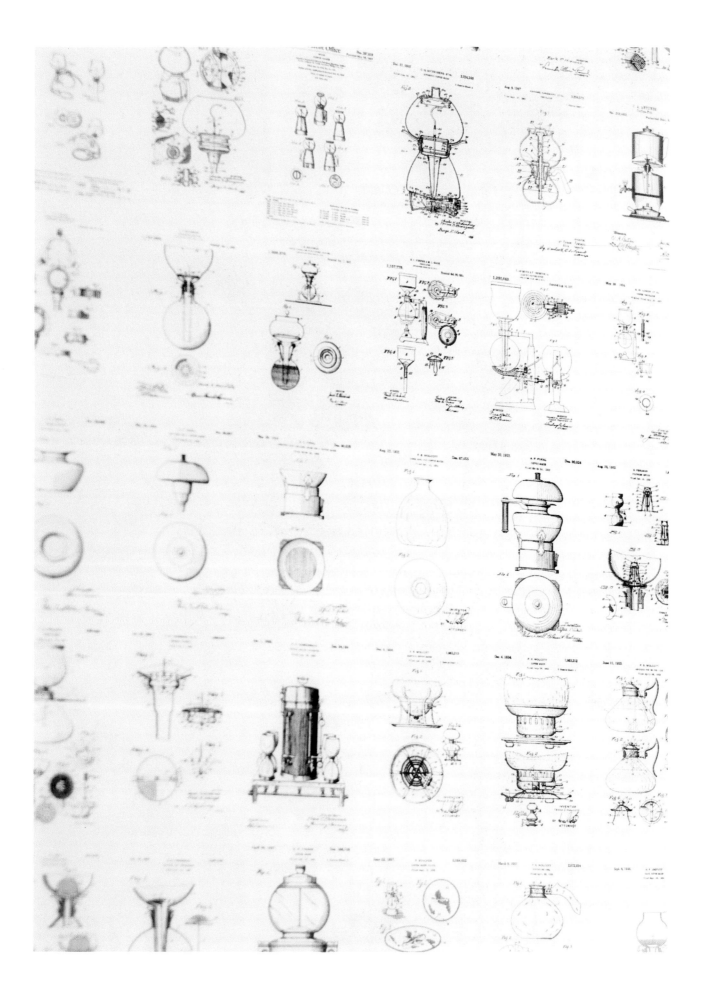

It's not the coffee that unfurls our minds and spirits, but the meaningful conversation that accompanies it.
It's not the coffee that lifts our eyes and awakens our bodies, but the time we take to make it.
And it's not the coffee that prepares us for the day, but the encouraging words from those we love.

SARAH LANG

LEAVING

Everything is not always as it seems.
Notice the patterns, stories, and movement going on around you.
When you start your day tomorrow, imagine each place you visit is new;
use all of your senses, and find a different world.

PHOTO ESSAY BY KATHRIN KOSCHITZKI

There is a character named Rafael in Michael Ondaatje's Divisadero who has a passion for cilantro. "His pockets always held a few herbs, basil or mint, so he could rip off a heel of bread and create a meal wherever he was." [4] *The space between him and his lover, before they'd kiss, filled always with the smells of his shirt pockets. This is part of what attracted her to him. Not cilantro-smelling kisses, but a resourcefulness, an imagination. His meals depended not on a table, but on available ingredients and amount of light. He ate on trains, in valleys, by streams, and under trees. There is a romance in this. For where we eat and cook, we are at home. The wider our variety of eating places, then, the bigger our home.*

NIKAELA MARIE PETERS

MORNING BAKING

A young baker recounts her early-morning routine and the affinity she has developed with her trade.

The hour is early and there is a calm quiet that I find comforting. Morning. Dough, flour, and sugar cover my workspace, evidence that it will be a good morning. Baking is now intuitive: after hours of prepping, researching, and practicing, I know that my hands, body, and soul have memorized each recipe. From the kitchen I can hear the barista dialing in, click, click, click—perfecting the grind of the espresso, pulling the first shot of the day, checking its taste. Notes of espresso fill the air and the regulars start to arrive.

As I place a dozen maple date scones into the oven, I hear someone ask about blueberry muffins, and I know without looking at the clock above my head that it must be six-thirty. The muffins are ready. Their sweet crumble is golden brown, and the dark blueberry juice escapes from the cracks: art, if you ask me. I place them on a slab of wood and head out to the pastry case. Their scent fills the café, catalyzing a group of customers to get up from working (drinking coffee) to order muffins. As I stand there, all but a half dozen are sold, and I take this as a sign that my hard work—and early hours—are worth it.

I was once a customer at the café, and each day I would look forward to the ritual of drinking my cappuccino. Then and now, I enjoy the café as a place where people can pause. Sometimes customers are in a rush, but the baristas, baked goods, and I encourage a slow atmosphere of conversation and appreciation. The baristas converse through the pour of each cup, the contrast of espresso to milk, their love of coffee evident in every movement. We encourage customers to appreciate their coffee slowly, to talk about the espresso, to discover subtle notes and flavors in their cup. Over time, customers become regulars, and begin to yearn for those conversations. They slow down automatically, leaving our café with far more than a cup of coffee.

This morning, I chat with one of the regulars about curing meat and the art of baking the perfect carrot cake. After our morning conversation he leaves with a large *latte* and a café staple: an orange cranberry scone. I can always tell when those scones are almost ready; the warm scent of butter and citrus, a scent that I find familiar and enchanting, fills the air.

Walking back to the kitchen I can see a shot of espresso waiting for me. I take a sip and close my eyes; it's rich, flavorful, and sinfully sweet. The scent of figs escapes the oven. Like the regular customers, I cherish routine. My mornings are defined by scones, muffins, espresso, and those slow and thoughtful human interactions that coffee shops allow. I place my cup down, wipe my hands on my apron, and roll up the sleeves of my soft flannel shirt. The morning has just begun.

WORDS BY CAROLINE EGAN & PHOTOGRAPH BY NIKOLE HERRIOTT
WOODWARE BY HERRIOTT GRACE

TWO

ENTERTAINING FOR TWO

○ ○

TACTILE COOKING

Cooking, while intended to fill bellies and entice taste buds, is also a tactile experience: chopping, kneading, noting temperatures and textures.

PHOTO ESSAY BY TEC PETAJA & STYLING BY CHELSEA PETAJA

MY AUTUMN PANTRY

Every cook has a favored season, and although I can mount a mighty compelling argument for spring, summer, autumn, and winter, the one for autumn rings most true. Shorter days, colder nights, an oven baking and broiling at full tilt, a heavy pot of stew on the burner—it's a wonderful scene to settle into each year. Here's what I keep at the ready...

Honeycrisp Apples	*Farro*	*Family-Sized Soup Pot*
Brussels Sprouts	*Oatmeal*	*Cookie Sheets*
Quince	*Wild Rice*	*Vintage Cake Pans*
Pomegranates	*Homemade Pie Crusts*	*Thermos*
Delicata Squash	*Loose Leaf Tea*	*Beeswax Candles*
Sunchokes	*Cast Iron Pans*	*Vintage Cookbooks*

WORDS BY HEIDI SWANSON & PHOTOGRAPH BY ALPHA SMOOT

WHAT WE CARRY IN COMMON

*Two sisters, bonded by blood and friendship, introduce their sons to
a childhood tradition of sharing fresh pastries.*

WORDS BY WON MCINTOSH & PHOTOGRAPHS BY ALICE GAO

Our ages don't matter. All that does is being together, small fingers stealing swipes of powdered sugar off the croissant, *crumbs dropping on the tabletop like some tender, familiar trail, the comfort of memory and of carrying it on.*

In the autumn that I was five, my sister was born. There were so many years between us that from the start we never really shared the same season of development. Those milestones of life that move us step by step from infancy to adulthood arrived at different times for each of us. I was off to school when she was learning to walk, and I was feeling the first flutters of a crush when she was just learning to make her own friends. I remember trying to teach her how to read. I remember leaving home for college and the way she buried her head under the covers the morning I left, too sad to speak to me. She wouldn't leave for another five years. Always I went ahead of her, and always she was catching up. But somehow, perhaps as a testament to her maturity (or my immaturity), we were—and still are—great friends.

Our mother helped us. She never made much of our difference in age. Instead, she would call us to the car and take us out for pastries. It was something we did about once a week. And though we went year-round, I most clearly recall our jaunts in the cold months—sitting together at a small table in a simple Japanese bakery, a pretty custard bun on a paper doily for each of us, a piping hot cup of coffee for our mother. My sister and I learned to love the smell of coffee early on, that smell at once of stepping into bracing air and of coming home again. We learned to love the comfort of sitting in a warm bakery, licking custard from our fingers, watching the fuzzy shapes of people passing outside the misted windows. We learned to love being together, no matter our ages, no matter our season.

We entered adulthood, and our experiences began to equalize. But it was the birth of my first child that suddenly propelled my sister forward, even as I was propelled newly into motherhood. She stepped ahead of me in a sense, becoming something I had never been: an aunt. Her nephew came in the autumn of the year she was married. She held him for the first time in the hospital, close to her heart. I loved her for loving him, especially in those early days when my own postpartum emotions felt tenuous. Three years later, I had another boy, and she held him too,

as closely as she had held his brother. Aunt and nephews adored each other easily, absolutely. They shared the same chin, the same love of cookies still soft in the middle, the same gleam of joy upon seeing each other again after a spell. I always wondered about that, about her ability to treat each time she saw them as though it were the very first.

Then, in the autumn that my oldest turned five, my nephew was born. My turn had come, and I finally understood what it meant to love your sister's child. Outside the hospital window, the East River flowed quickly, eager and churning, the glints of sunlight that fell on its surface floating away without pause. Inside the room, it was as if everything—my sister laughing, my brother-in-law holding up a camera, my boys dancing around my husband— paused for a moment while I met him. "Hi. I'm your auntie," I said. He looked at me, one eye shut, one eye tentatively open, taking his time while taking me in. It was like I had known him a long time. Where love for your own child looks constantly forward, the love that you feel as an aunt is steeped in memories, the happy ones from childhood, of warmth, of togetherness. I nuzzled his forehead, and he smelled faintly—of all things—of custard.

It feels like the coldest day in February when we enter a cheery glass-front bakery in the West Village. My boys climb onto chairs and swing their legs back and forth. My sister removes my nephew from his carrier, and he smiles at me. Though I get to see him at least once a month, each time is indeed like the very first. My boys try to tickle their cousin. He blinks, surprised, then considers them curiously, unaffected by clumsy appendages ruffling his tummy. We order—to share—a chocolate *croissant*, a cherry cream scone, two sticky buns that glisten like jewels. We get cups of coffee for ourselves. We are mothers now, and aunts. Our ages don't matter. All that does is being together, small fingers stealing swipes of powdered sugar off the *croissant*, crumbs dropping on the tabletop like some tender, familiar trail, the comfort of memory and of carrying it on. ○ ○

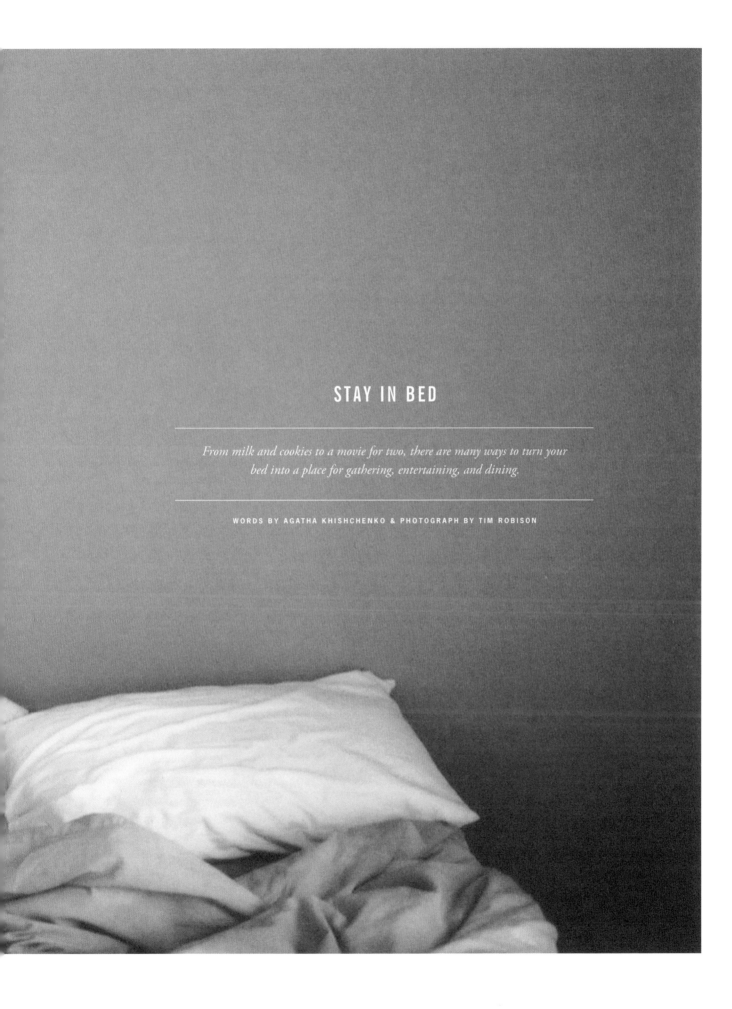

STAY IN BED

From milk and cookies to a movie for two, there are many ways to turn your bed into a place for gathering, entertaining, and dining.

WORDS BY AGATHA KHISHCHENKO & PHOTOGRAPH BY TIM ROBISON

BREAKFAST IN BED

The sun streams through the window, awakening us with its warm rays. I sink deeper under the duvet and glance at my sleeping partner before rousing myself out of bed. Hair tousled and pajamas rumpled, I pad into the kitchen and begin my weekend ritual of grinding coffee beans, toasting bread, and soft boiling eggs. Arms laden with a tray full of breakfast, including steaming mugs of creamy coffee, I climb back into bed, eager to dunk buttered toast soldiers into runny yolks. A sharpened pencil stands at attention, ready to tackle the Sunday crossword. The morning hours stretch leisurely ahead of us, a sign the weekend has arrived.

A SURPRISE INDOOR PICNIC

Unexpected rain showers cause a picnic to be reinvented indoors. A plaid blanket draped over the duvet, gingham napkins, and a handful of wildflowers turn our bed into a private indoor picnic. We lean back on plush pillows while nibbling on the accoutrements that were wrapped lovingly in our basket: cold roasted chicken salad and red-skinned potatoes cloaked in a creamy herb-flecked aioli. We sip from pony-necked beers. Slices of pound cake and watermelon are a sweet ending to our impromptu indoor picnic.

MILK AND COOKIES

Nothing conjures childhood like a glass of cold milk and a plate of cookies. Bedtime meant an evening treat, listening to fairy tales while nibbling on cookies or biscuits. Occasionally a neat row of Oreos would appear, inviting us to plunge them into glasses of cold creamy milk. We would snuggle under blankets and quilts, a plate of cookies balanced on our knees, begging for just one more chapter to be read aloud. Our parents would smile, patiently sigh, and always succumb to our request: just one more story, one more chapter. Today, a plate of cookies, a mug of tea, and a novel make for a familiar bedtime treat.

MOVIE FOR TWO

The threat of a snowfall entices me back to bed. While a movie choice is debated, a menu forms— savory olive-oil popcorn, sliders, salted-caramel sundaes—decadent options but fitting for such an affair. We each sip a Negroni while preparing our spread, debating who will win the Oscars this year. A touch tipsy, we dim the lights, slide under the covers, and cue the film. Movie night has commenced.

URBAN CAMPING

While I love backcountry camping, some of my friends are not as eager to rough it in the great outdoors. We decide to bring the experience indoors. Sleeping bags are spread in the bedroom, a flask is passed around, a friend strums a guitar, and stories are shared. The room is lit by candlelight, which we use to melt marshmallows onto graham crackers and bars of chocolate, the urban camper's version of s'mores.

LONDON CALLING

Avid tennis fans think of Wimbledon as the epitome of the season's tournaments. The time difference means the serious matches are aired just as daylight breaks on the East Coast of the US. Alarms are set, tea is brewed, and we watch the finals while partaking of the traditional Wimbledon breakfast: strawberries and cream. Between sets, we slather preserves and clotted cream on scones and rush to the kitchen for cucumber-and-cream-cheese sandwiches. Wearing our best pajamas 3,500 miles across the Atlantic Ocean, we sit in bed, ardently cheering on our favorite players, and hoping next year we will be there to watch this spectacular event live on Centre Court.

SICK DAY

As a child, I secretly relished catching a cold because it meant I could stay home from school, reading Nancy Drew while my mother brought me meals in bed. A runny nose and fever meant chicken soup: a hearty broth that my mother would boil for hours and fill with sweet carrots, potatoes, and cauliflower. A sore throat meant a cool bowl of ice cream or hot tea with buttered cinnamon toast. (For my Chinese friends, ginger, scallions, and *congee* were *de rigueur* when one took ill, and my Italian friends would eat bowls of warm *pastina* sprinkled with *parmesan*.) As an adult, staying home alone doesn't hold the same magic as before, but I make do, brewing tea, toasting bread, or if all else fails, ordering in hot soup. Flannel pajamas, a thick duvet, and my warm puppy snuggled at my feet make staying home a pleasurable experience. ○ ○

APRON RECIPES

The messes that prove our time has been well spent. Indeed, a filthy apron is the lingering memento of those who properly express themselves in the kitchen. Take note, reminisce, then launder.

PHOTO ESSAY BY GENTL & HYERS

Affogato

Pizza

Heirloom Applesauce

Pickled Beet Salad with Goat Cheese

Cardamom Ricotta with Pistachios and Honey

Chocolate Soufflé

FEW

ENTERTAINING FOR A FEW

○ ○ ○

THE LOST COAST

A group of friends travels to the Lost Coast—an undeveloped section of the California North Coast—for remote surfing and campfire cooking.

WORDS BY NICHOLAS J KOCH & PHOTOGRAPHS BY ALEX FARNUM

As our SUV skidded along the muddy clay road toward the trailhead, the rain fell violently, blindingly, our car shuddering as storm winds swept over us from the Pacific Ocean. Our surfboards were sardined in the cargo bed behind us, flanked on either side by rattling bottles of beer and camping equipment. I scanned the radio dial; a voice crackled through the speakers, announcing that the storm was expected to last two days—the exact length of our trip.

We had organized the trip far in advance, knowing we were risking bad weather. As the trip neared, we realized we were heading straight into the middle of a furious coastal storm. Despite the less-than-ideal conditions, though, the four of us were in high spirits; this was the first time in months we had gotten away from

perhaps even a trip or two through the storied California desert. But, as often happens, the demands of daily life interrupted those plans. Not long after signing my first lease, I was foisted into a management position at my job, which, along with my twice-weekly stints as a bartender, swallowed up all my free time.

And just like that, five frenetic years somehow blurred by me, my initial reveries of outdoor exploration lost in the chaotic shuffle of an unforgiving work life. As 2012 rounded the bend, I found myself disheartened, repeating old resolutions to work less and frolic more, resolutions that I only half believed I would uphold. And then, as my friends and I were enjoying the sun of an unusually warm February afternoon, they mentioned an overnight surf-

<hr>

SUGGESTED DINNER MENU

DUTCH OVEN CORN BREAD
Baked over hot coals—pg. 88

CAMPING CHOPS
Marinated during hike into camp—pg. 97

SPICY BITTER DANDELION GREENS
Harvested wild—pg. 96

GRÃO-DE-BICO
Portuguese style chickpeas—pg. 138

<hr>

our apartments and our neighborhoods and our wearying jobs. The prospect of getting a little soggy wasn't about to sour our moods. We pulled into what we hoped was a parking spot and filed out of the vehicle, the rain relenting to a manageable drizzle as we prepared for the modest two-mile hike to our campsite. We were in the heart of California's Lost Coast, and, with my friends guiding me, I—a novice outdoorsman—was about to fumble my way through my first surf trip.

The Lost Coast is a nearly-one-hundred-mile swatch of coastline five hours north of San Francisco, a mecca for hikers, campers, and surfers. When I moved to San Francisco in the spring of 2007, I did so in a fit of whimsy, abandoning the piss and vinegar of New York for the promise of California's sunny, adventurous lifestyle. I'd had visions of Pacific-side hikes and leisurely bike tours through wine country, and

camping trip planned for April. I had never so much as held a surfboard, but they invited me along all the same. I agreed without hesitation.

Now we swiftly made our way along the rocky trail that led to the cabin, surfboards tucked underneath our arms and packs jangling on our backs. By then the sprinkling rain had stopped, and the sun was peeking through the grumbling storm clouds as if to welcome us. Before long, our cabin rose into view, perched at the top of a verdant hill overlooking the Pacific. It looked more like an early-century barn or granary than it did a campsite. It was a stately vision of deteriorating Americana whose wooden slats were faded gray from decades of sunlight and salty ocean winds. Inside, the sleeping area was small but beautiful: two sets of wooden bunks sat on either side of the room, and a west-facing window afforded us a view of the heaving Pacific Ocean. We settled in quickly,

continued on page 92

DUTCH OVEN CORN BREAD

RECIPE BY CHRISTINE WOLHEIM

Freshly baked bread over an open fire? It can be done! I recommend you make this easy and mix all the dry ingredients in bag or jar before you go, essentially making a corn bread kit. You'll need a cast-iron Dutch oven with a tight-fitting lid, so this is perhaps a better recipe for car camping, but when you are in the great outdoors eating hot corn bread with butter and honey, you'll know it was worth the effort. Besides, it's fun to make! *Serves at least 4.*

COMBINE BEFORE YOUR TRIP	AT YOUR CAMPSITE
1 cup stone-ground cornmeal	1 cup milk
1 cup all-purpose flour	1 egg
⅔ cup sugar	⅓ cup of vegetable oil
1 teaspoon salt	
3 ½ teaspoons baking powder	

METHOD Before the sun goes down, you will need to scout around for three rocks about equal size and about four inches high. After your fire has formed some coals, place the three rocks in a circle, in your fire pit but not right beside the fire. You want to rest your Dutch oven on top, and have it be stable, but also have room to funnel hot coals into the center of the rocks. The goal is to have a heat source under your Dutch oven, but *not* have it actually touch the coals—remember, we are "baking." Spread a nice layer of coals in the middle of the three rocks, and around them as well.

Combine the dry and wet ingredients of the corn bread mixture into a bowl, and stir only enough to mix (this will keep the corn bread tender).

Place the Dutch oven on top of the rocks, and get it hot but not smoking. Remove from heat. Swirl a small amount of the vegetable oil all around the inside of the pot, then immediately add all the corn bread batter. Cover and return to the rocks on top of the coals.

Using a shovel, cover the top of the pot with as many coals as you can. Do not bury the pot; you just want to add some heat to the top. If one side of the pot is exposed or close to the main fire, rotate often. You want the coals to do the cooking, not the fire. Try to maintain even coal distribution under and on top throughout the cooking process. Check for done-ness every 15 minutes or so. Because this is not a yeast batter, you can take the lid off without fear of your bread falling. You will know it's done when it has set in the center, and lightly springs back to the touch. You may need someone to hold the flashlight for you while you check!

Pull the Dutch oven out of the fire, remove the lid, and turn it over onto a clean cloth or plate— the corn bread should come right out. Serve with butter and honey or use it to sop up all the lamb sauce. You'll be lucky if there is any left for breakfast!

spilling our belongings onto bunks like dogs marking territory, and began stepping into our wetsuits almost in unison, all of us eager to take advantage of the break in the foul weather. We were ready to see what kind of surfing the Lost Coast had to offer.

The path leading from the cabin to the water snaked picturesquely through the seaside hills. It dropped steeply from the campsite's bluff, through a copse of eucalyptus trees, and finally onto the narrow, rocky beach. We waded into the ocean one after the other; I, the least experienced by a large margin, brought up the rear, my surfboard leashed awkwardly to my ankle. The water was cold, but not

in catching anything resembling a wave, and, even then, I was never able to rise from my belly. But as I was out there drifting on my stomach, partially immersed in the brisk northern Californian ocean, my friends' voices wafting to me over the waves, I couldn't think of any other place I'd rather be.

We arrived back at the cabin wet and chilled and tired and tremendously happy. The storm, in all its previous ferocity, seemed to have abated, even if just temporarily. We leaned our boards against the warping planks of the cabin's walls and clambered back inside, the sunshine warm on our backs, and we carefully peeled off our wetsuits and rubbed our numb hands together.

To witness a seasoned surfer catch a respectable wave,
gracefully maneuvering the surfboard as if it were an extension of his own body,
as if the curling drums of water underneath him were something he could control—
to see that happen is a thing of beauty.

---

uncomfortably so. The Lost Coast, however, is no bunny hill—the waves were choppy, frenetic, upset by the intermittent storm. I paddled about halfway between the stony shore and where my friends had clustered, content to simply bob in the waves and watch them surf.

To witness a seasoned surfer catch a respectable wave, gracefully maneuvering the surfboard as if it were an extension of his own body, as if the curling drums of water underneath him were something he could control—to see that happen is a thing of beauty. Every fluid movement represents years of devoted practice, years of the trials and errors and injuries and improvements and defeats that simply come with the territory when learning to do something you love.

I tried once or twice to catch a satisfactory little tumbler, but I lacked the grace of my comrades; I only succeeded a handful of times

Once we were all clothed and dried, I pulled out the corn bread batter I'd brought with me, and, taking my cue, each of my friends followed suit. One by one, their respective contributions to the family meal appeared—lamb chops, dandelion greens, the makings of a chickpea stew, and an impressive array of alcohol. I stepped out of the cabin to start the fire as everyone set to preparing supper; I could hear the others sharing stories of surfing triumphs and calamities while they chopped and sliced.

As I stood next to that ancient cabin, the unexpected sunshine waning into dusk, I thought of how I got to this rocky seaside trail, of those blurry years that whisked by. I smiled to myself as I peered out to the Pacific, the sounds of clinking bottles and laughter floating out of the cabin and into the salty coastal air, like waves. ○ ○ ○

SPICY BITTER DANDELION GREENS

RECIPE BY CHRISTINE WOLHEIM

Anyone who has gardened knows how insidious dandelion is. The best revenge is to eat big heaps of this very nutritious green. It grows wild throughout most of the US, and can be easily harvested. Many farmers' markets now sell it as well, and if you buy the greens, you may wish to wash them before your trip so they will be ready to throw into the pan. *Serves 4.*

⅓ cup good olive oil
3 cloves garlic, peeled and crushed
1 teaspoon dried crushed chili flakes

1 large (or 2 small) bunches dandelion greens
salt to taste

METHOD Have your greens ready, washed and roughly chopped. Over an even bed of coals, heat a large skillet, and add the olive oil and the garlic cloves. When they have browned on all sides (take care not to burn), add the chili flakes all at once. Allow to toast and further scent the oil (do not allow to burn or the mixture will become bitter).

Immediately add the dandelion greens and sauté them, stirring frequently, for 8–10 minutes.

You may add a little water if needed. These greens are hearty and can be cooked down or eaten *al dente*, depending on their maturity and your personal taste.

They make a nice complement to the lamb chops and corn bread. Bitter is better!

CAMPING CHOPS

RECIPE BY CHRISTINE WOLHEIM

It's a good rule of thumb is to have two T-bone style lamb chops per person. They can be cooked directly on the fire, but this method yields a nice, rich sauce in which to dip your corn bread. *Serves 4.*

PREPARE BEFORE YOUR TRIP	AT YOUR CAMPSITE
8 T-bone style lamb chops	4 cloves garlic
good olive oil	sea salt or kosher salt
freshly cracked black pepper	8 sprigs of fresh parsley
1 large sprig rosemary	good olive oil
	1 ½ cups good red wine

METHOD Before leaving home, place the chops in a large plastic bag, drizzle with oil, and sprinkle with the cracked black pepper. Strip the leaves off the rosemary and place in the bag as well. This will serve as a marinade for several days; keep the meat in a cooler until ready to use.

When ready to cook, remove chops from bag and discard rosemary. Place chops in a shallow dish; peel and sliver the garlic and rub into the meat. Salt the meat generously. Pluck the parsley and sprinkle on top. Toss all together.

Over a medium bed of coals, heat a skillet. Add approximately ⅓ cup of olive oil. Sear the chops on both sides until well browned, about 3 minutes per side.

Deglaze with the wine by adding the wine to the pan all at once. It will bubble up—don't be alarmed! Move the pan to a place on the fire where it can simmer for a minute or two (you may wish to check and remove the chops at this point to avoid overcooking, as per your taste). When the wine has reduced (cooked off by at least half), and combined with the meat juices and oil, you will have a luscious sauce. Pour over the chops, and serve immediately.

SUPER POWERS

*A simple moment at a fish cart sheds light on the difference between
an old life and a new, powerful one.*

The realization that I had changed came on a quiet afternoon, at a restaurant here in Rome. The waiter listed the names of the fish available that day; I smiled and told him I had no idea what those fish were. He offered to show me. But at the cart, I named each fish as he pointed to it, the words rolling off my tongue. He laughed and told me I had it under control. I guess I did, but I was surprised that I could identify a whole fish, something I didn't recall learning.

I rewound the tape in my head. I reviewed all the experiences I'd had in food shops, and I almost missed what I was looking for—I had to roll my memories forward and backward, the way you search for a specific scene on a DVD. There it was, in my fairly recent adult memory: the fish counter. Lots of ice and lots of precut fillets. Then I rewound much further, to my childhood, when the fish was breaded and in rectangular sticks. I could attribute my previous ignorance to life in Nashville, a landlocked city—but really, I suspected it was more about life in America. Many of us like our food already cleaned for us, just the way we plan to cook it, keeping the best parts (whatever we think those are) and discarding the rest.

I've heard that when you lack one of your senses, the others become more heightened to compensate. When I moved to Italy, I lost the retail food outlets that I was used to in the United States, and I had to find new-to-me ways to procure and make the food I wanted to eat.

Today, in addition to being able to identify whole fish, I know how to trim artichokes, the quick way to remove the middle rib from kale leaves, and that you can use the entire leek, not just the white part. I know how to cut a whole chicken into parts—in fact, I own two pair of poultry shears. I also own fish pliers and tweezers and can remove the pin bones from salmon before making *gravad lax*. I have a drawer of special tools I never imagined I'd own, and I now think of foods and dishes by season, looking forward to the months in which they will be at their peak. I know that I have to catch fruits and vegetables in their window, or try again the next year. I have learned how to select produce and how to make so many things: curries, dumplings, Tex-Mex, a full Thanksgiving dinner, the perfect burger, all things American, and of course Italian. I have conquered savory and sweet baking, dropping by the pastry shop for tips from the pastry chefs from time to time. I have also realized that it is extremely empowering to be able to prepare from scratch whatever I want to eat.

At the fish cart that day, I wondered how I had made it so long without knowing what are, at the end of the day, the most natural things to know. I now think of all of these bits of knowledge as my new "super powers." While I feel extremely capable and greatly strengthened, a part of me is ashamed at having been so "weak," but I won't dwell too long. Instead, I have started to teach my husband what I have learned, beginning with the basics.

WORDS AND PHOTOGRAPH BY KRISTINA GILL

ESSENTIALS OF FALL CAMPING

*A weekend with friends at a lake house or cottage can be a marvelous way to
usher in and embrace the cooler days of fall. Follow these simple tips to guarantee
a well-documented and aesthetically satisfying trip.*

PHOTO ESSAY BY SARAH & CHRIS RHOADS OF WE ARE THE RHOADS

WORDS BY JASON HUDSON

PACKING LIST

1. Visit your favorite local shop with companions to purchase coordinating clothing. Ensure there are no competing plaids or bossy colors.

2. Carefully wrap all of your tableware and vintage accessories, and place in a large suitcase.

3. Remember that when venturing into the forest, tobacco pipes are critical. Fingerless gloves are optional.

STONE SKIPPING

1. Find a large, calm body of water.

2. Photogenically toss a smooth, flat stone toward the lake while looking intensely handsome. Results unimportant.

PROPER CANOE TECHNIQUES

1. Only participate should an attractive canoe be available. See also: hand-carved oars—while heavier, these photograph beautifully.

2. No other tips; just wing it.

GAME PLAYING

1. The best amusements are those with neutral patterns, which won't distract from the beauty of your surroundings. Grotesquely colored games, those fashioned out of plastic, or the variety not recognized by our grandparents are strictly *verboten*.

2. Have fun!

LAYERING FOR FALL

1. Because the weather this time of year can vary wildly, please layer accordingly. While all types of chambray and plaid are encouraged, do avoid bright, joyful tones.

2. When choosing jeans, the tighter the better—though take care not to tear while hiking, skipping stones, or climbing down into low-slung canoes.

SWEET POTATO BUTTERNUT SQUASH SOUP

INGREDIENTS

1 medium butternut squash

3 ½ pounds sweet potatoes

3 cups chicken or vegetable stock

½ cup half-and-half

½ onion, minced

2 cloves garlic, minced

3 tablespoons coriander

1 ½ tablespoons curry powder

1 tablespoon chili powder

pancetta for garnish

salt and pepper to taste

soft goat cheese for garnish

chives for garnish

METHOD

Serves 6.

Preheat oven to 425°F. Cut squash in half, clean out the seeds, and place facedown on foil-lined baking sheet. Place whole sweet potatoes on the same sheet.

Roast until squash and potatoes are soft, approximately 45 minutes. Once cool to the touch, remove skin and place the flesh in a large soup pot. Add stock and half-and-half. Stir until incorporated.

Add onion, garlic, coriander, curry, and chili powder. Bring to a simmer and maintain for 10–15 minutes, stirring often.

In a small sauté pan, cook *pancetta* over medium-high heat until done, approximately 5 minutes.

Using an immersion (or traditional) blender, puree soup until smooth. Salt and pepper to taste.

Garnish with soft goat cheese, chives, and cooked *pancetta*.

Serve with a thick country loaf. *Pictured on page 114.*

Recipe by Jenice Lee

PUMPKIN BUTTER

INGREDIENTS

3 cups pumpkin puree

¾ cup dark brown sugar

1 cup apple cider

1 teaspoon cinnamon

½ teaspoon nutmeg

½ teaspoon ground cloves

METHOD

Yields approximately 4 cups.

Combine all ingredients in a large saucepan and bring to a boil. Turn down the heat and let mixture simmer for 30–45 minutes, giving the flavors time to combine.

Stir often and taste, adjusting the spice according to your preference.

Store in an airtight container in the refrigerator for up to a week.

Recipe by Jenice Lee

HOMAGE TO CHEESE

Cheese, while delicious, also has a storied past and a cultural significance that we may not often consider.

WORDS BY KIRSTIN JACKSON & PHOTOGRAPHS BY GENTL & HYERS

We know that cheese, like wine or sugar, is a force.
Its flavors seduce us and address our most basic desires and evolutionary needs.
It helps to bring people together and support communities.

Occasionally, when it's time to tell someone I make a living from touting the glories of fermented milk, I pause. Although I can only think of a couple things I'd rather do than sip bourbon while teaching students about southern cheese and spirits, or travel around the country visiting creameries, petting baby animals, and sampling fledgling wheels, researching my upcoming book on domestic cheese, I know that there are still people who don't see beyond the yellow and white cheese bricks sitting on their grocery store shelves. While I see cheese as a rich, nourishing, cultural, and historical food whose milky beauty has inspired legions of food photographers, to some, artisan cheese is little more than protein, fat, and sugar in a pretty package.

Despite any initial hesitation, my love for artisan dairy and reaching its future disciples means I must reveal my calling. When I do, most people smile and say they dream of having access to the many pounds of cheese I try not to consume every week. Then there are the few non-believers who don't understand what there is to study—and they are why we forge ahead. Professional cheese lovers like me believe it is only a matter of time before these people realize that artisan wheels are far more than just nutrients covered in a shapely rind.

We know that cheese, like wine or sugar, is a force. Its flavors seduce us and address our most basic desires and evolutionary needs. It

helps to bring people together and support communities. It can serve as an instrument that allows cheese makers to make their mark in the socio-economic sphere, and it is a creative, artistic outlet that helps bring beauty to everyday life. With so much going on in every wheel, it's not hard to understand why people already feel so connected to cheese, and how those who don't already, will.

First, cheese exerts its power by blindly seducing us on physical and emotional levels. Melted on a pizza or served with crusty bread, cheese speaks to our most basic and subconscious culinary desires. The first food to quiet our earliest cries was mother's milk. Take that milk, make it even richer, sweeter, and saltier—in cheese form—and you have a connection to your earliest emotional and social bonds. But you also have something that strikes evolutionary chords. Our ancestors sought sweet, rich foods that delivered ample energy so they could provide for and protect their family units. Today we subconsciously seek out the same things, and cheese is one of the lushest, energy-delivering foods out there. Cheese: sensory points galore. Us: defenseless.

Cheese also helps people survive beyond offering nutrition—it binds communities together, forms important alliances, and provides a commodity. For example, in the ninth century, French families in the Franche-Comté

With so much going on in every wheel, it's not hard to understand why people already feel so connected to cheese, and how those who don't already, will.

region who didn't have enough milk to make large wheels of Comté for the winter didn't just make smaller wheels. They formed cooperatives, pooled their milk, centralized cheese making and aging, and redistributed the wheels in their community and beyond. This tradition is still the norm today.

People in the United States also support themselves and provide for their community by making cheese. When milk prices dove during the recession, most dairy farmers across the nation were unable to break even by selling their milk. But by making cheese from it, some were able to sell their product at artisan cheese market prices rather than fluctuating milk market prices, which are dictated by stocks and government oversight. There were some people who didn't even own farms that began making cheese to support dairy families and independent farms in their community by buying their milk. Fermenting milk became a way to keep farming communities alive, and more dairies every day consider turning their milk into cheese, to battle the constantly fluctuating milk market prices.

For others, making cheese is a means to live outside of the prevailing socio-economic norm where larger farms (most selling heavily government-subsidized soy or corn) can have a much better chance at making a living while smaller farms constantly struggle. Growing what you want, and how you want, is difficult when you have to compete with heavily subsidized products in the marketplace. Cheese can provide

security. Producing it on the side can help farmers build a financial cushion—so they can grow that buckwheat they're really passionate about, or afford to keep the animals they adore. That extra cheese money just might allow them to have the animals they like, or grow what they want, how they want to grow it, on their farm.

Then there are people who love making cheese because it's a beautiful creative outlet. Cheese nourishes, brings communities together, and allows people to farm the way they want, but it is also an art form. Although making cheese is hard labor, it is a craft that brings pleasure to both its creators and its admirers. Sometimes the rinds alone take one's breath away. Brainy, wrinkly, ashy, smooth, waxed, covered in cocoa nibs or espresso or tiny divets, they show a loving touch like a cut of fabric on a quilt does. In some ways, cheese's beauty—an already pleasing exterior giving way to layers of texture and flavor within—serves as a metaphor for its variegated reach and role in our lives.

Perhaps everyone's eyes don't light up yet when they hear I work with cheese for a living. Maybe they haven't yet met the right cheesemonger, one who will inspire their dairy desires, or their passion has not yet ignited by knowing that they're consuming a product that has provided beauty, focus, and shape to so many lives and communities. But I have faith that they will. The cheese bug can bite when it's least expected, and it's hard to resist such a delicious force when its effect is so sweet. ○ ○ ○

SHARING PESTO

Preparing for seasonal cooking with a garden's basil harvest.

We arrived at our mother-in-law's house with the essentials—olive oil, nuts, garlic, and cheese. She greeted us in her flowered apron, glasses of wine in hand to share. The smell of sweet basil and the laughter of other guests floated past the dining room as we emptied our baskets onto the table. She led us to her sun-drenched patio where we carefully pulled fresh leaves off the basil stalks, an overabundance from our friend's garden, preparing to make our first batch. With the basil ready we went back inside and gathered around the table, each at our own little station. We dipped bread into a bubbling skillet of Fontina and garlic and enjoyed fresh pesto pizza from an earlier batch. Processors started whirring and the hum became the background to laughter and conversation. As batches of pesto were finished, they were stored in jars for the fridge or spread on wax paper and shaped into logs for the freezer. In the coming months, slices will be cut from these logs, ready to add to any dish. As the evening quieted down, the floor was swept of fallen herbs and the dishes were scrubbed clean. A wonderful summer harvest was shared with dear friends.

WORDS BY BETH MURPHY & LARISSA MURPHY

PHOTOGRAPHS BY CARISSA GALLO

INTERVIEW: JENNIFER CAUSEY

*Jen Causey, creator of the Makers Project, tells of its inception and the intense
pull she feels toward the artisans and craftsmen she meets.*

INTERVIEW BY JULIE POINTER & PHOTOGRAPHS BY ALICE GAO

WHAT INSPIRED YOU TO BEGIN THE MAKERS PROJECT AND HOW LONG HAS IT BEEN GOING ON? WAS IT A NATURAL TRANSITION TO TURN THE PROJECT INTO A BOOK?

I started the project almost two years ago. It began out of curiosity. I have always been drawn to people who make things with their hands and I loved the idea of getting a closer look through documenting them. It was also a way for me to grow a bit as a photographer and to explore things I was not currently doing in my professional life. My primary focus at the time was more objects-based, shooting food and still life, mostly in a studio. The project has allowed me to mix things up and photograph more people—real people—with objects, in their natural environments. This has bled over into my professional life and I am now shooting more lifestyle work, which I love!

When I was approached by my editor to turn the project into a book, it was something I had thought about before, but not seriously. I am really happy that the photos will have a permanent, tangible home together in a book.

WHERE DO YOU THINK YOUR FASCINATION WITH MAKING AND MAKERS STEMS FROM? HAVE YOU COME FROM A LONG LINE OF HANDS-ON DOERS AND MAKERS?

Growing up, my mom was always baking, gardening, and crafting, and my dad was always building something. Creativity and making were always encouraged, but never thought of as a career path. I think this is why I became so interested in this rise of people making things for a living that was happening around me in Brooklyn.

A MAKER'S WORKSHOP CAN BE A VERY PERSONAL SPACE; CAN YOU THINK OF ANY FAVORITE OR INTRIGUING DETAILS THAT YOU'VE LEARNED ABOUT SOMEONE JUST BY BEING INVITED INTO THEIR WORKPLACE?

By visiting these studios and workshops, I have seen the hard work and dedication that goes into hand-making things. It is exhilarating to listen to makers talk passionately about what they are doing. One of my favorite things about the visits is looking around the studios, searching for unique trinkets and hidden treasures. When I was photographing the Saipua flower studio, the first shoot of this project, I remember seeing a jar of everyday rubber bands sitting on a shelf next to two tiny vases. It was a perfect little work of art living on the shelf. I love when an object is both beautiful and useful. This has since become one of my favorite photos from the shoot.

WHAT IS THE MOST REWARDING PART OF THE MAKERS PROJECT FOR YOU?

I love seeing the growth in the makers I have photographed. It is amazing to see them get more public recognition and to see their work get better and better. Another reward is wearing something from makers I have photographed, or enjoying foods or drinks made by them. I get a sense of pride when I get compliments on my Odette necklace or my Fay Andrada bracelet. I love recommending Makers' products to people, as I know firsthand what went into making it.

HAS THERE BEEN A FAVORITE FEATURE YOU'VE DONE OUT OF ALL THE PEOPLE YOU'VE INTERVIEWED? OR A FAVORITE SPACE TO PHOTOGRAPH?

I have loved photographing each and every maker! They have all been so generous in letting me into their worlds. That being said, I really loved photographing Erin Considine's jewelry studio. I love the way she mixes metal and textiles, hand dyeing all her fibers using natural dyes. She is doing such original work with such history and integrity behind it. And her studio gets amazing light! ○ ○ ○

AUSTIN, TX

WORDS BY JULIE POINTER & PHOTOGRAPH BY KRISTOPHER ORR

We gathered in a century-old pecan orchard just outside of Austin, Texas, for a simple evening picnic at the outskirts of Johnson's Backyard Garden. As the light faded and the spring heat mellowed, we enjoyed food fresh from the fields around us, met new friends at our makeshift table, and listened to acoustic tunes played by Texas's own Balmorhea. Austin's close-knit community of makers and artisans spoiled us with pies, honey, cider, coffee, and other such treats, gifting us with more than we could possibly devour in one evening. We were honored to enjoy some sweet southern hospitality.

SAN FRANCISCO, CA

WORDS BY JULIE POINTER & PHOTOGRAPH BY LAURA DART

O ur San Francisco brunch was a whirlwind of flowers, fresh market goods, delicious food, and lively conversation, all shared at Heirloom Café on an uncharacteristically fog-free day. We deemed the gathering to be farmers' market–inspired, and our partners overwhelmed us with a generous outpouring of gifts for our brunch guests—including everything from walnuts to bouquets to soap. As you might expect in San Francisco, we left feeling well-fed, inspired by the wealth of creative individuals we met, and encouraged by the evidence of thriving local businesses.

PHILADELPHIA, PA

WORDS BY JULIE POINTER & PHOTOGRAPHS BY PARKER FITZGERALD

We were privileged to gather at the beautiful Terrain at Styer's for our Philadelphia dinner. We shared one communal table in the barn, surrounded by summer's early blooms in the gardens. Guests enjoyed a delicious seasonal meal made with ingredients from a variety of local farms and purveyors, and had the pleasure of sharing the table with some of our evening's partners—farmers, winemakers, butchers, and coffee and tea experts, among others. We found our Pennsylvania hosts and attendees refreshingly down-to-earth, gracious, and welcoming, and enjoyed our time spent lingering in the gardens with new friends.

PEAR TARTLETS

PHOTOGRAPH AND RECIPE BY ERIN SCOTT

These pear tartlets taste like autumn, mingling herbaceous, sweet, and savory flavors all at once. They can easily be packed for a breakfast in the woods, or enjoyed for a late afternoon tea by the fire. If you are taking these tartlets to go, wrap up the cooked shells and place them in a container that will protect them from breaking. Pack the compote in a lidded jar. Bring a spoon for the compote, and plenty of napkins. *Serves 4.*

SHORTBREAD CRUST

5 tablespoons unsalted butter, melted & cooled

⅓ cup golden honey

1 ½ cups almond meal

1 teaspoon almond extract

2 teaspoons fresh rosemary leaves, chopped

⅛ teaspoon sea salt

PEAR COMPOTE WITH HONEY & BAY FILLING

3 ripe pears (2 cups), peeled, quartered, & cut into thin slices

1 tablespoon lemon juice

1 bay leaf

½ cup golden honey

4 small sprigs of rosemary for garnish

METHOD / SHORTBREAD CRUST Preheat oven to 350°F. Mix all ingredients in a bowl until well blended. Using your fingertips, press dough into the bottoms and sides of four 5-inch tart pans (buttered or nonstick). Use the tines of a fork to press about a dozen holes into the surface of the crust.

Place the tart pans directly on the middle rack of your preheated oven. After 10 minutes of baking, the crusts should be poked again a couple of times with a fork: this will keep the dough from bubbling up too much. Continue baking for another 5–8 minutes, until the crusts are deep golden brown. Let cool. If you aren't going to eat right away, you can leave on the counter for a few hours until you're ready. They should be eaten the day they are cooked. Serve at room temperature.

METHOD / FILLING: PEAR COMPOTE WITH HONEY AND BAY Combine all ingredients in small saucepan. Bring to a boil. Cook vigorously, at just below a boil, for 10 minutes—until the compote has thickened, and the pears have maintained their shape and not become mushy. Stir regularly to avoid burning.

Pour compote into a jar and let cool to room temperature before serving. If you aren't going to eat right away, cover your jar and refrigerate until ready.

When you're ready to serve, scoop pear compote into the shells. Top each tartlet with a sprig of rosemary, just for the beauty of it. Take a bite, and let the pear juice drip down your chin.

GRÃO-DE-BICO

RECIPE BY KRISTINA TOSI (PORTUGUESE-STYLE CHICKPEAS)

It's best to make these beans ahead of time, then warm them over the coals in a camp pot when you're ready to eat. You could also make them at your campsite, but someone will have to tend the fire (to maintain the right temperature) and stir! You should have some leftovers, which would be wonderful with breakfast. *Serves 4 with leftovers.*

½ pound chickpeas
¼ pound *linguica*, cut into bite-sized pieces
1 medium onion, chopped
2 small garlic cloves, minced
1 ½ teaspoons salt

2 tablespoons red wine vinegar
1 tablespoon chili powder
a few sprigs of thyme
1 bunch of kale, rough chopped

METHOD Wash peas, then soak overnight in enough cold water to cover them. Drain and rinse peas and place in large pot or Dutch oven. Just cover with fresh cold water.

Add sausage, onion, garlic, salt, vinegar, chili powder, and thyme sprigs. Bring to a boil.

Reduce heat to low, cover, and cook for 3 hours or until beans are tender. Halfway through, add chopped kale. *See corresponding story on page 83.*

SPECIAL THANKS
Paintings Katie Stratton
Art Director at Weldon Owen Ali Zeigler
Production Director at Weldon Owen
Chris Hemesath

HERB DRYING
Pictured Skye Sarenana-Velten

WHAT WE CARRY IN COMMON
Location Peels NYC
peelsnyc.com

APRON RECIPES
Ceramics Marcie McGoldrick Design
marciemcgoldrick.com

Aprons provided by:

Terrain
shopterrain.com

Society
societylimonta.com

Libeco
libeco.com

Stich & Hammer
stitchandhammergoods.com

LOST COAST
Food Stylist & Recipe Developer
Christine Wolheim
Stylist Lisa Moir

FALL CAMPING (RHOADS)
Photography & Directing Chris & Sarah Rhoads
of We Are The Rhoads
Food Styling Jenice Lee
Wardrobe Lisa Moir
Cinematography Joel Clare
Props Scout Vintage
Location homeaway.com
/vacation-rental/p321653
Unionmade
Pendleton Portland Collection
Herschel Supply Co.
Cottage Farm Etsy

CHEESE STORY
Ceramics Marcie McGoldrick Design
marciemcgoldrick.com

Styling Angharad Bailey
angharadbailey.com

Cheese Bedford Cheese Shop
bedfordcheeseshop.com

ENDNOTES

1   Michael J. Gelb, *How to Think Like Leonardo da Vinci: Seven Steps to Genius Every Day* (New York: Bantam Dell, 1998), 97.

2   William Allingham, "Day and Night Songs," *Flower Pieces and Other Poems* (London: Reeves and Turner, 1888), 106.

3   Honoré de Balzac, *Physiologie du mariage, ou, Méditations de philosophie éclectique sur le bonheur et le malheur conjugal* (Paris: Charpentier, 1847), 34.

4   Michael Ondaatje, *Divisadero* (Toronto: Vintage Canada, 2008), 74.

BACK COVER QUOTE CREDIT
Heidi Swanson for *Kinfolk*

**THANKS TO OUR
DINNER SERIES PARTNERS:**

AUSTIN, TEXAS
Anja Mulder
Any Style Catering
Argus Cidery
Austin's World of Rentals
Balmorhea
Blackbird Bakery
Black Lodge Coffee
Canoe
Contigo Austin
Farmhouse Delivery
Folk Fibers
Houndstooth Coffee
Johnson's Backyard Garden
Josh Loving
Kristopher Orr
Loot Vintage
Nouveau Romantics
Robert Mondavi Private Selection
Salt & Time
Tiny Pies
Type A Press
West Elm

SAN FRANCISCO, CALIFORNIA
Apolis Global
Batter Bakery
Caroline Egan
Danamark Nuts
Enjoy Events Co
Farmgirl Flowers
Fleurish Events
Floral Theory
Heirloom Cafe
Heritage Public House
Jarlsberg
Jered's Pottery
June Taylor Jams
Laura Dart
Living Greens
Mrs. Meyers
Noteify
One True Love Vintage Rentals
Redwood Hill Farm
Revival Vineyards
Ritual Roasters
Samin Nosrat
St. Clair Brown Winery
Star Apple Edible Gardens
Studio Choo
Tartine Bakery
Type A Press
Wayfare Magazine
West Elm

PHILADELPHIA, PENNSYLVANIA
Anja Mulder
Apolis Global
Art in the Age Craft Spirits
Blue Moon Acres
Brown Betty Desserts
Galer Estate Wines
Happy Cat Farm
Jarlsberg
Lilikoi Design & Letterpress
Nest
Parker Fitzgerald
Philadelphia CowShare
Rachel Koppenhaver + Rachel Hosan
Sea Chant
Spodee Wine
Sullivan Owen
Teaspoons and Petals
Terrain at Styer's
West Elm
Wild Flour Bakery
Woolwich Dairy

WWW.KINFOLKMAG.COM

KEEP IN TOUCH